THIRSTY FOR GOD'S PRESENCE

by K.R

It's 2023 and you're...

unemployed

unvaccinated

single

a felon

tired

unmotivated

stuck

ashamed

thirsty

...just as blessed as anyone
with breath in their body

This book is dedicated to people young and old who don't have anyone in their lives that pray for them, which is upsetting to imagine but truly exists because that's what we have turned this world into. I pray for them, all of my brothers and sisters in Christ, everyone who doesn't know Christ and to all those people who are no longer with us since their souls will live on just like ours are going to. May God's will be done

FOREWARD

I have had the pleasure of getting to know K.R. over the last couple of years. I have heard his heart as we have talked about the things of the Lord. In this book, he shares aspects of his personal story. He writes with transparency in addressing some matters of a personal nature. He desires to connect with the reader on a level that will make an eternal difference.

He pours his heart into his writing. He speaks of his personal relationship with his Living Savior. He conveys his beliefs in an easy to understand manner that will be a help to one that is not currently on the same faith journey that he is. But, this story also takes the reader on his life's journey that will serve to affirm for current believers of our faith.

Over these past couple of years, K.R. has spoken encouragement to me as we have talked about matters of life. He has aptly titled this book, Thirsty for God's Presence, as that has been his desire – to be close to the Creator of all; and walk in obedience to His Word. He has spoken words of life, love, and truth into my life. And he accomplishes this in the telling of his story. I am honored to know K.R. as a Brother-in-Christ. And I count it a privilege to have been a witness to this journey he has traveled.

-Minister J.T Clark of VA, author of "My Brother's Crossing" and the movie of the same name

I saw a rainbow today that made every aspect of living more than okay. I feel marvelous. Not because I am struggling to find my way, not because yet again I have managed to ruin what I thought was true love, not even because I feel free and no longer have a care in the world. It is because God made a promise to me saying He would handle it whatever it is. I just need to have faith, I do. He's the reason why I don't have those cares or worries. He's my real true love and I'll serve Him amen

-K.R

REMEMBER...

What we all have in common is that we are sinners saved by grace. No sin we've ever committed can stop us from receiving God's mercy. Even when mankind (society) judges you, looks down on you and doesn't want to give you a chance, you are blessed. Anyone looking down on you is judging you and anyone who judges will be judged. Anyone who does not forgive will not be forgiven and those words from the Lord are clear as crystal. When all you have is Jesus, you have all you will ever need. Believe and receive Him and all your downs will turn up. What you have lost will be reestablished or you will receive double for your trouble. That's the kind of God I serve and He wants to do so much for you.

LOST LOVES

There will be peace in the valley for me one day

Unfortunately, we live in a sinful world. The most profound consequence of this fact is that death comes knocking at every door. Most people have lost a loved one at some point in their life and if they haven't, they will. I currently am dealing with a recent loss that really shook me because I was just with this person weeks prior. The immediate lesson I learned from this experience was that I have to send that text. Take that call. Make that visit while I still can.

I've never been a person that handles death well so I've never been to a funeral and my first wake was my last. I was fourteen at that wake. The viewing of someone I knew personally, lying in a casket stuck with me to the extent where I never returned. I've missed grandparents', uncles' and cousins' funeral which led to me having to deal with family members being upset with me for not attending. I've prayed on it and I know prayer works because years ago I used to pray that the Lord never take loved ones away from me, I even asked Him to take me before any of my family members died because that was how strongly I feared losing anyone. Of course He didn't grant me that request but what He did do was even better.

God helped me grow strong enough to deal with death and to look at it from a different perspective. I now understand more than ever that when a person like my friend Blair passes away, they are heading to a much better place than the one we are in now and that way of thinking is how I have become better equipped to handle the losses that are multiplying. I was hit with two heavy losses just last year and asked to be a pallbearer for both. Imagine that, I went to my very first and then my second funeral a few months apart. Although I was nervous I happily accepted the offers to serve at the going home ceremonies and asked a few loved ones what exactly my duty was for the position I was offered. I cannot think of anyone I would have rather broken my string of avoidances at funerals for than you Pee Wee. You were truly a great one. I was blessed to experience your love and it was an honor to serve you in that capacity. I will serve you even more in the coming future. Mother Joyce, your death came suddenly. It was the shortest amount of time someone passed since the last time I saw them, literally one day. I was rocked uncontrollably. You touched many lives in your lifetime and the output of condolences and support via social media, the funeral and repass is proof. I am glad to have had you in my life and your joy lives on through your sons, entire family and everyone who knew you well. I hope to see all those who have gone ahead in the next life. There will be peace in every valley one day.

FEAR

What is the fear of the Lord?

One of the biggest questions/confusions I had was about fearing God. In my younger years, the God I learned about from the Old Testament seemed like an angry, violent God who punished everyone when they did wrong. I didn't see any loving quality from Him at all yet I wasn't afraid of Him most likely because I was too busy being afraid of my mother and other frights children obtain. Looking back now, I can see how wrong I was and that's what studying the Word is all about.

Each time I reread a scripture I learn more. Each time I read the words inspired by the Father in Heaven, my spirit stirs in a way only He can create. As an adult, what I've learned about the God from the Old Testament is that He's the same God in the New. Constant disobedience by God's people was always met with constant forgiveness. Ever since the great flood brought a new beginning, God has been showing us mercy that carried over to His Son our Savior. He is the God of another chance. Still, what eluded me was why He wanted us to fear Him. Many peers of mine that struggle believing in Christ have some of the same concerns that I myself have had. Mainly, it seemed to me that either we do what God says or we go to hell. I didn't understand how that could be free will. The more I read the more it was made clear to me. Yes, the understanding He promised was given and the scripture was proven once again. God cannot lie. As I type this I tell you with full honesty that it was last night when I finally understood what to fear the Lord really means.

Fearing God comes in many forms and I have chosen to speak about three: respect, awe, submission. Respecting God as the creator of Heaven and Earth and of all life will lead to us showing a great level of reverence to Him in our every day. Fully grasping Him as the reason for the seasons, the stars in the sky along with the moon and sun in addition to all knowledge that has ever been established will leave us in awe of His magnificence. Keeping both those in mind makes it easier to praise Him, give Him all honor and to glorify His holiness. Full submission by surrendering yourself to His will, asking for it while praying to Him is all a part of fearing Him. The fear of the Lord is the beginning of wisdom. Only in Him can we have true peace so it is wise to not do wrong by Him.

UNEMPLOYED

*Do not withhold good from those to whom it is
due, when it is in the power of your hand to do so*

We're living in very turbulent times. No matter
where you are in the world, life isn't as wonderful as
we would like it to be and it's evident. I cannot con-
vince myself to watch more than the first few min-
utes of a news segment. I hardly watch television
period unless sports are on. It saddens me to see
the hate, violence, starvation and natural disasters
that are continuously being broadcast. What really
bothers me is when one person or group or compa-
ny or country is fully capable of making change in
the lives of others but fail to do so. This is sadly the
case no matter where you turn. Nationally, in my
home country the U.S, many are suffering without
signs of an end. One of the biggest problems plagu-
ing the country is unemployment. Yes, the COVID
crisis has a lot to do with it but unemployment has

been a crisis long before then. There are some caring individuals who have showed up to aid those in need and I will continue to do what is in my power to do as well. Part of that is spreading the message I am spreading. When we are in the position to help someone and don't do it, we are setting ourselves up to fall to that same fate.

If you believe in God, you know God sees all. If you believe He doesn't hold us accountable when our brothers and sisters are in need but we don't do our best for them, you are mistaking more than I have ever seen someone make a mistake. When we give freely we will be richly rewarded. Don't frown your face at another because you think you are better than that or you think they deserve it. What they deserve is your support because you never know what a person might be going through. Even if you do, that gives none of us the right to judge or mistreat. For the record, turning someone away who is in need when you can help them is a form of mistreatment. So to those who are unemployed I say-don't give up and look for twice as many jobs as you would be able to handle while also keeping the faith. God will move someone who will then move your situation from hopeless to promising. I know from experience which is why I'll never take the break I received for granted. It is a real blessing when you are put in a position to help someone in need. God gives us these opportunities often and I always am humbled when I can make the littlest difference for another. I wouldn't be where I am now if it weren't for the support I received so I always want to give back no matter how difficult my situation might be. God rewards obedience so talk to Him like you would talk to someone sitting right next to you. Ask Him to fill you with His Holy Spirit. The Holy Spirit is a gift to us and through it we can reach our highest selves. It is a process that takes obedience and patience so day by day focus on a growth that only comes through your walk with Jesus.

A MOMENT AWAY...

I don't worry about tomorrow I live now; no debating on whether now or later is the time to get right for the Lord

Tomorrow isn't promised so why would I worry?

If you aren't ready now, knowing Jesus could return at any moment then you are taking the biggest chance ever taken in the history of chances

I won't leave that to fate

I won't roll that dice

I've never been much of a gambler

I'm preparing now

FELONS

*Forgiving others is the most Christ-like
act we can carry out*

Over and over, again and again throughout time human beings have done evil in the sight of the Lord. Just like generations of past we today continue to let God down yet He continues to bless us as we call to Him, forgiveness. What a mighty God! We are unworthy. God loves us so much that He grants us mercy through His Son Jesus. How long will we repeat the same sins against God? We're not promised tomorrow to once again repent (just saying).

God's kindness is intended to lead us to repentance. His kindness extends to everyone including lawbreakers. No matter what you have done or what has been done to you, depending on the Lord so that you can release it by growing through it is the answer. Yesterday cannot be had again so whatever happened yesterday has to be left there. You can still be your best you. This goes for everyone; you WILL NEVER BE YOUR BEST YOU if you do not forgive others what they have done to you.

None of us are perfect so we also must forgive ourselves. I struggle with that more than I ever struggle with forgiving another. When I do not forgive myself, I too hold back blessings because I am saying I don't have faith in God when I hold on to past transgressions. God has forgiven it all so who are we to hold on to it? What I know is I want to be the best me I can be and I want to accomplish all that the Lord has in store for me. There is no way for me to do it if I don't let go of what was. Even if others don't forgive me and don't want to see me do well, they have to answer to God for that. Meanwhile, I can't be stopped by anyone except myself. Moral of the chapter is to help others for Jesus' sake, even if they can never return the favor.

THIRSTY

I'm thirsty for God's presence, so more and more I call out to Him knowing He will not delay is always on time.

Paul, a persecutor of Christ and His followers turned major writer of the New Testament, was imprisoned in Rome. He wrote many letters and one was of encouragement to Timothy, his pupil. He didn't complain from behind those bars; he shared excitement and anticipation. He was looking forward to being with Jesus. He was undeserving of imprisonment but was told from the beginning of his transformation that he would have to suffer. So when I do wrong and I suffer I should be even more inclined to accept it and praise God anyhow! Life is a day to day struggle that has to be won day to day. satan is always in the midst but God is always in the blessing business. It's a war we can win only through Christ. Therefore, let the one who boasts, boast in the Lord.

The kingdom of God is not a matter of talk it's a matter of power. **I will call upon Him as long as I live,** God my driving force. **Are you thirsty for change and more importantly, are you thirsty for the Lord in your life?** You break the cycle when you turn to God!

A MOMENT AWAY 2

"Who can this be that even the wind and sea obey Him?"

I'm not concerned if the words I fall upon are as beautiful to the next person as they are to me because there's no comparison. I'm just a young kid from a diverse town who didn't think much about the Lord outside of the Bible animated series that my grandmother used to make my cousin and I watch (I love you Shanequa). It is God alone Who saw what He saw in me because He put it in me. I had my own plans and Lord knows I have messed up all of them. He also knows what it will take to steer me where He wants me to be and I want to be there because I believe with all my heart that it is the best place for me to be.

That Word my, that Word. It's almost unfair how good It is. The more I read the more I am in love with It. The more I read the more I want to read and as I keep reading I keep re-falling in love with It. It has changed me and saved me so many times. The Lord is the best part of my life and when I read about the many times He was the best part in the lives of His servants from the Bible's lives, I get this glow from within. The Bible is full of inspiring stories, people who came from the lowest of lows or were mistreated deservingly or undeservingly. I think back to all God brought me through, I can recall just thinking- "This is it. I'm never going to recover from this," but He was there. Right there. Came to rescue me. That's love yeah that's love and don't be misinformed because if you ever had instances like that in your life in which you don't know how you survived look no further.

—— Prayer

Lord I come to you as humble as I know how.

Still, if I need be even more humble allow me to learn. This is more of a prayer so I assist that effort by going down onto my knees.

I thank You for all that I am and for being my Lord, Savior, Friend and Father. If I had a thousand tongues I couldn't thank You enough for

Your love and Your grace and truth be told, I don't deserve these blessings

You give to me. Over and over I try to figure out why it is You love me. I feel as if I'm unworthy of Your love truth be told again, I'm not.

That's why I praise Your name. That's why I must keep You first. My love for You shall never end so render me the opportunity to serve You.

Give me the wisdom and the understanding I need to succeed because there is no one that can fill me with joy like You. Therefore, no one deserves to be worshiped but God. You truly are the best part of my life. Thank You for making me worthy through Jesus the Christ. Amen

Don't Allow Anyone to Take Your Crown

(read the book of Ephesians)

In 1 Peter chapter 2 verse 9, Peter tells us that we are "a chosen people, a royal priesthood, a holy nation, God's special possession." Before accepting Christ Jesus, we are not a people. Once accepting Jesus, we are God's people receiving mercy by being brought out of darkness so that we may praise Him who showed us grace.

The first line of that verse stands out to me because of the spiritual connection I make to it. Being chosen, becoming royal in this sense is not only a holy royalty but it is the greatest form of royalty one can possess! This is not man-made royalty based on tangible or tarnishable positions and items. Through Christ Jesus we share in eternal glory and honor! Being that this is a gift and cannot be earned, this also means it cannot be taken away from us without our permission. This is where we ourselves can be our worst enemy by the decisions we make:

Do we accept this truth and walk in it? Do we continue to live less than by our choices including willingness to give satan a foothold, meaning an opportunity to cause disruption in the peace we can obtain? The book of Ephesians not only tells us who we are in Christ, it also tells us about the many ways we give invitations to the devil and how to avoid doing so.

Gratifying the cravings of our flesh

If you don't know by now, we were all born in sin. Every single human being to ever live was born a sinner outside of Christ Jesus and Adam & Eve, who brought sin to us by their decision to disobey God. With that being said, there will always be a battle between our spiritual being and our fleshly, human being. It is a war we cannot win by ourselves and more times than not, I find myself losing this battle when I try to fight it with my own knowledge and ability. Whenever we use our own limitations in the effort to succeed where we are completely out-matched, we fall short and may even become discouraged. For myself, that discouragement can lead to giving up and giving in to what I feel is wrong but somehow justify, proceeding in that direction. This is where the gratification of our flesh begins to give satan a foothold.

Now in Christ Jesus, you who once were
far away have been brought near by
the blood of Christ

These are some of the sweetest words ever written. I can make the argument that since we were born in sin (by no choice of our own), that it is only right that we are saved from sin (not by our actions but because of God). However, that doesn't cover the other fact of the scenario we call life. As we grow older we learn right from wrong and we still make decisions that go against our teachings. There are even some instances where we may go into a situation knowing how wrong it is but we do so anyway. The gratification mentioned above. Nevertheless, no matter how long we have done wrong, no matter how long we have knowingly done wrong, one man who none of us can be remotely like on our best day, has given us an opportunity to do just that! Why? Because we are loved by His Father and we are loved by Him! You were bought with a price and you are of special value. Who? Anyone who accepts Him as their Savior.

No longer foreigners and strangers, but fellow citizens with God's people and also members of His household

What this means is that no longer are we far away from the kingdom. It is as near as being inside your body. Being a believer and follower of Christ doesn't just end there. You become a citizen of Heaven. You have the title of being one of God's people; you are a member of His precious home. I'd like to call that beauty

In Him you too are being built together to be-
come a dwelling in which God lives by His Spirit.

Having God near you comes through the advocate which is the Holy Spirit, His Spirit. Once we
accept Jesus we are gifted that Spirit and once we
have that Spirit we begin to be built up into a place
God will not only dwell but He will make known
to others this new light in your life. That is how we
serve part of the purpose God has us here for, to
bring others to Him as well. God is the Creator. Jesus is the Savior. The Holy Spirit is the advocate and
intercessor working on our individual behalf.

Through the gospel the Gentiles are heirs
together with Israel, members together of one
body, and sharers together in the promise in
Christ Jesus.

Israel being the chosen people of God received
all His promises, His faithfulness, love and protec-
tion. Because of disobedience and lack of apprecia-
tion for the Father, this led to God's grace and mercy being extended to anyone anywhere in the world
who turns their life to Him. That major promise of

eternal life is now for everyone who accepts Jesus which also turns us into one body. We are one body in Christ and are set apart for a purpose.

We may approach God with freedom and confidence.

...because we are set apart and because we are in Christ, we should walk with a certain confidence that breaks every chain that has been holding us down or holding us back. We are free from it all. When you know who you are in Christ then you know that whatever you ask of God who is the Father of us all, He will provide or guide you to receiving. Do not, however, allow this confidence to become arrogance or entitlement.

Be completely humble and gentle; be patient, bearing with one another in love. Make every effort to keep the unity of the Spirit through the bond of peace.

Peace is the key word here. Keeping the peace as far as it is up to you. Avoiding conflict or chaos. Bear with those who you KNOW are not where you are trying to get to spiritually. In our effort of being pleasing to the Lord, we must understand that part of that is how we deal with people, whether agreeable or disagreeable people. Showing that you are living for Christ and not yourself is where the gentleness, the patience and humbleness are able to excel.

Grow to become in every respect the mature body of Him who is the head, that is, Christ.

I am grateful to God that I now know that it is the disagreeable people, the adversity and the trials that are the blessings in disguise. We cannot grow to be more like Christ if we don't experience hardships, tests and setbacks. We must suffer with Him to reign with Him. What kind of reigning will we do? God is the king of kings. The Lord of Lords. The first and the last so take a guess

Having lost all sensitivity, they have given themselves over to sensuality so as to indulge in every kind of impurity, and they are full of greed.

This verse is an example of what happens when we become too full of ourselves. We may very well reach a highly successful position in life through our service to God and unfortunately we may also let our guards down and begin to forget where we started and who is the reason for where we are currently. We may even reach a point where what God has done for us is not enough so we want more and in order to get more we become both carefree and careless. We live as if we can do no wrong. We live as if no one else matters therefore how we reach the goal we set out is by any means necessary. This is very dangerous because of the harm it can cause to others and another point the self indulging individual should think about is- this road will certainly end at a self-destruction like none other, courtesy of the King.

Do not let any unwholesome talk come out of your mouths, but only what is helpful for building others up according to their needs, that it may benefit those who listen.

..therefore it is important to stay on guard against yourself and others who may lead you astray. In both cases, satan is at work and when we aren't watching what we say and do, it becomes much easier for us to fall to our human nature. I only want to build others up; Lord knows I do. That is what this book is about and my life's work moving forward. It goes back to what I believe to be true: we are of one body.

Get rid of all bitterness, rage and anger, brawling and slander, along with every form of malice. Be kind and compassionate to one another, forgiving each other, just as in Christ God forgave you.

These are the works of the flesh, our human nature. This is the darkness that is ever present in this world and at any moment can attach itself to us if we are not careful. Jesus Christ mastered the fight against these malices from start to finish. This is part of the meaning to Him being "The Way." Only with His help can we master this, the Holy Spirit. So while we go through life learning not earning God's grace (because it is free), take time out to meditate on these words and all scripture. Life was never promised to be easy but what is promised by God is a way to withstand it all. We must recognize the attacks, especially those coming from people we will least expect and expect some to come out the blue too. I've heard so many times that if you stay ready you won't need to get ready and I believe that to be true. Being proactive may be a more common definition and that is the way we must be in the spiritual realm as well. Let us equip ourselves in all these ways for those moments that can easily bring us down. Let us get to a place where when those moments arrive, we simply stand strong, take the blows then adjust our crown.

UNMOTIVATED

"Shall we accept good from God and not trouble?"

No one that I found in scripture spoke to God so boldly and freely as Job. A true man of God, he was obedient to the point of praying for mercy for his disobedient children. He lost all of his possessions and those very children, along with his good health all because satan wanted to prove God wrong. Though I've heard many preachers suggest Job never wavered in His faith or curse God, Job did let out his anger and desire to die because he couldn't understand why the God whom he served had abandoned him.

There will be times in everyone's life (no matter who you are) when you lose motivation or a will to carry on. You might even know someone who took their own life because of a circumstance they saw no coming back from. They couldn't have been more wrong just like satan couldn't have been. Job waited for his chance to speak with God directly and once it was given he immediately realized his mistake. Since you are still here now I want to tell you with no more delay, there is always a way when it comes to the Lord and Savior Jesus Christ, Son of the Most High God and the Holy Spirit they grace us with. So don't lose heart when you receive blow after blow. You can go toe to toe with any obstacle if God is on your side. Pray without ceasing and learn the Word if you don't already, that way you can stay in the fight and cause your troubles to flee. We gain power through the Holy Spirit immediately after turning our lives over to Christ. And how do we do this? By saying 'Lord, I know that I was born a sinner. I know that I need You to save me. I ask You to come into my life and change me into what You would have me to be. Your plan for my life is the best plan. You died so that I can live. Please, enter into my life and help me renew my mind.' You have to know what you want, visualize it, close your eyes for a few seconds each day and see yourself having all God has in store for you. Although you may not believe it now, He has special plans for you and when I say "you" I mean every single living human to ever have lived. But He won't force Himself on anyone. Anyone that believes in Jesus receives forgiveness in His name with love. Jesus is the way the truth and the life. He's the Alpha and Omega and He's coming soon.

A MOMENT AWAY 3

Somebody asked me how I could serve someone that I've never seen, never heard.

I disregarded that person went home that night and told You why I love You God. "Because of You I am smiling. Because of You I'm not sad. Because of You I have noticed life isn't so bad. Because of You I am saved.

Yes I mean that rebirth. Because of You I am breathing air on planet Earth.

It's all because of You why I'm making it not faking it. I'm free I am me. I am strong I am wise. I haven't met my demise. I am Yours You are mine because of You my light shines."

Later, I went back to that same person to answer the question for them

"How can I love Him?" The Lord has spoken to me. I see Him in all

Christ followers. Best yet, I can feel Him deep in my heart and He is strong."

See God it's because of You that I have the nerve and readiness to explain what it is we have going. You are simply the best and that's simply put

STUCK

The Lord does not change

Seasons change, feelings for one another change but God never does. He also never has. He is the same now as He was yesterday and will always be. That is good news for all of us but what isn't good is when we don't change our old ungodly ways. We are gods, He says we are. We are told to be holy because He is. The only way to do this is through the Holy Spirit which has been promised to us once we accept Jesus as God's Son our Savior. It won't happen overnight, but doing so will allow you to let go of regrets, heartache and whatever you might be holding onto that is deterring you from becoming a new creation.

For me, letting go of the past has never been more necessary. Never having my biological father in my life didn't begin to affect me until I was an adult. Why? I don't really know. I never knew him and he was gone before I ever could so I'm left with a 'what if' that sometimes drives me to madness. It's not what God wants for me. So I had to get out of the habit of feeling sorry for myself for never having a father.

If that wasn't enough heartache, I am dealing with the fact that I don't have a strong relationship with my mom. She disappointed me in many ways and again, it didn't begin to affect me until I was grown. I hold a fear of her that I don't want to get into. What is most important and crucial is that I thought I did but it's clear I haven't yet forgiven her. God forgives and gives us multiple chances, always has always will. Who am I to not do the same? God knows that I want to forgive and because I asked Him to help me I know that I will reach that plateau. In this weakness I pray He makes me strong but this isn't my only weakness needing healing

I'm single not because I want to be. I haven't yet figured out why I ruin relationships but I've been told several times over that it stems from my relationship I had with my mom (or lack thereof.) Whatever the cause it has caused me to hurt several people mainly by my words. Yes this tongue is a raging fire that has been hard to put out. So although God doesn't change, we must change our sinful ways especially when they are causing hurt to others. Those bad habits also block what God has in store for us. Through prayer and supplication it is possible to change.

And the way I was able to stop feeling sorry for myself for never having a father was when I realized that God is my Father and He has always been with me.

—— PRAYER 2

You have put joy in my heart my Lord, blessed me in more ways than there are numbers. I shall fear none other none other matters because I have You. You alone my Lord are more than enough reason for me to smile more, a while more, be strong helping and holy. Reveal Your righteous words so that I can be found in them again and again. I want to serve You. I want to spend my life doing Your work. My work is Your work, that is what I want it to be. That is what I want to do, Your work. You have put joy in my heart and You saved my soul with your Son Whom I love and need. Now that I have You encourage me to keep You. Help me to the best way I can.

ASHAMED

There is only love, and it covers all sins

Since the Lord always has a plan for us despite what we are faced with, we must seek Him in all circumstances including disappointment.

Shame is included in that. No matter what you have done, NO MATTER, God is love and only love can set you free from your demons. Only you have the power to stand strong against opposition and anyone who wants to hold what you have already been forgiven for against you. Now, you're only forgiven after you genuinely ask Jesus from your heart to forgive you and to help you not sin again. That last part is very important. The way you activate the power inside of you is by mediating on the Word and humbly in prayer. God can free you from whatever is holding you back and bring to you whatever you are seeking. He has healed the sick. He has allowed the blind to see. He has helped the lost be found. He will set you free but it will be done in His timing not yours.

God certainly blessed Joseph for all the mistreatment he received on behalf of his brothers. It is one of my favorite stories in the Bible and I believe in my heart all of the scriptures are true. Some people may say: God probably blesses and changes the situations of His servants that are unjustly afflicted. Besides the fact that we were all born in sin and shaped in inequity, Paul whom I mentioned earlier first had to be converted because he was responsible for some of Christ's servants' deaths. Paul fought against the Lord before fighting for Him and that change could have never happened if he wasn't forgiven first. God's love covers us all and is free to receive. Ask

UNVACCINATED

*And where the Spirit of the Lord is,
there is freedom*

We are all free in Christ because the Word says we are. Using our freedom to indulge in fleshly desires is still and will always be sin. God doesn't expect us to be perfect. He does expect us to lean on Him and not our own will. We are powerless without the Lord. We are more than conquerors with Him. After loving and honoring God, the next most important commandment is loving each other. We have to honor each other support each other and respect each other's decisions. So if you decide not to get vaccinated I respect you still. I believe you should pray about it and allow God to lead you to the right decision but I won't bash you for it. No one should be bashed for making a decision that isn't sin against another. You have to understand a person and their reasoning for doing whatever it is they do. Pray for that person and love that person while never disturbing their freedom in the Lord.

SEEK AND FIND

What my studying has taught me

The difference between accepting Jesus and following religion is that the latter focuses on human achievement. Accepting Jesus is the only way into Heaven. Building a personal relationship with Him is what is most important. The leaders in the church are supposed to help you accomplish this by pointing you in the right direction. My pastor always told me to read the scriptures for myself along with listening to sermons. There are no changes in what God requires from the Old to the New Testament, He just made a way for us to do what we were never going to be able to do on our own.

The testing of your faith produces perseverance. What this means is God can take our problems and use them for good. Problems are more likely to lead us to God for help. God is opposed to the proud but gives grace to the humble and problems will surely humble us. Your faith can be strengthened during problems of any kind. The stronger your faith is that the Lord will turn it around, the more He will turn it around for you. "Lord I know that this problem is not too hard for You and I know that You will see me through in Your time. Your time is always the perfect time." Tell yourself that and believe so that it is done. Just by asking the Lord to have His way, you are keeping the faith and that is when He will bless you.

The person who delights in the law of God and meditates on it day and night will prosper in whatever he or she does. This includes surrendering to His way, right down to how we live day to day. Humble yourself by acknowledging you are in God's hands and He is the One who promotes and exalts. God honors complete obedience and surrender but keep in mind, it will never be you doing it. It will be God living in you. That last line is key because if you are like me, you may be asking- 'what does full surrender actually look like? How do I fully seek Him?' By His grace. Once we accept Jesus Christ as our Lord and Savior, He then takes over. The Holy Spirit is so important so I will continue to circle back to it. The Holy Spirit intercedes for us; it is the advocate on our behalf and provides us with all we will ever need until Christ returns to be with us Himself. The Holy Spirit will help you completely seek and surrender to the Lord. This all occurs because of God's love for us.

—— PRAYER 3

Lord, please help me see clearly. Help me follow You confidently. Help me to not have a heavy heart when faced with complications. My feelings often get in the way and I ask You to help me act in a holy manner so that I don't miss the lesson or the blessing. In Jesus' name amen

A MOMENT AWAY 4

Christ is yours if you want Him

This goes for everyone, He loves us all

Just abide by and focus on the Word not what you heard

If you don't think you need Him then I will pray for you, and He will show you that you do. There is no one on this Earth like the God above

He created no one the way He did His Son, Jesus Christ and what a friend we have in Him!

HAVE, not had, because He is still with us all

Don't believe me? Call on Him really call on Him and really have faith. Keep it. Then you will get to watch the wonderful work the Lord does. Why live any other way when God's way leads to everlasting life with no worries? I believe God is coming and this Earth as we know it is going

Are you going with it because I'm going with God

I've made up my mind

—— PRAYER 4

Dear Lord,

I don't want to continuously act off of what I feel. I want my life to run through my faith in You. Forgive me for letting negativity have power over how I feel think and live. Thank You for Your Word which is everlasting love. It is only by Your grace that I am able to walk a righteous path and I shall continue to strive for that one step at a time. In Jesus' name Amen

TIRED

The safest place for us will always be inside of God's will.

God knows when we've had enough. God can tell when we have hit rock bottom. Sometimes it's what it will take for us to turn to Him before it's too late. I can testify to that because it happened to me. I was on the fence for so long although I knew God and what He expects of me. Sometimes I was in some-times I was in the world again. It doesn't work like that. The greatness of God and His love is He knows who belongs to Him. He has plans for us all. So as I continued on my path of destruction He stepped in and changed my life forever. When I had nowhere to turn I turned to Who I knew could see me through and I was right. God showed me not just once but many times that when I've had enough and I cannot take any more of my suffering, He will step in and handle it as if it was never there to begin with. The best part about it is it helps my belief in Him grow and I can turn to Him sooner the next time I begin to go astray. By doing this I access a power within me that is greater than the world because it has overcome the world! Everyone yes EVERYONE can have this access. Anyone that accepts Jesus as Lord and Savior receives forgiveness for every shortcoming and sin. You also receive everlasting life when He returns to establish His kingdom. This is the only way; HE is the only way. Jesus is the Alpha and the Omega, the beginning and end who will be returning soon! I will repeat that truth until there is no more breath left in me to do so.

Whatever worst-case scenario is trying to steal your peace right now, just know that God is in total control and holds our very lives in His hands. Even though people may fail you or you fail them, some may even have abandoned you but God never will. God can always see the best in you even when others only see your flaws. He has never failed me once and all of my strength comes from Him. I rest in that truth so that I can truly trust God. It gives me a boost and gets me up in the morning on those days when my tank is empty or my spirit is down. When I am weak, He makes me strong. Be less concerned about what you can or can't do and call on God. The more you do this, the more you become convinced about what He can do because He is going to show you.

God doesn't always give us what He has for us right away. He knows whether we are ready or not so this is why we trust Him. It is also true that He will never allow us to be tempted beyond what we can handle. We have to be patient through it all. Count your blessings even when you don't know what they are because if you know God you know He is always working for the good of you. Count those blessings and flip them by blessings others.

A MOMENT AWAY 5

I will get lost in God's Word all by my lonesome. Just like I will go if I have to go by myself, I learned that from Reverend Hubbard years ago. My praise will be heard loud; silence will be foreign in my life when it comes to glorifying my Lord. I will give thanks forever because God is my all. No one else comes close to being close. My trust is in the Lord fully. I'm keeping faith so satan you need to get behind me bully! God has kept me from the invisible net you try to capture me with. God has made me aware that He is my protector so He will keep me from your grasp.

I know my Redeemer lives. At the end I will see His face.

photo credit courtesy of Pastor Kevin Ford

A CHURCH FAMILY
reintroduced

You will always be loved by God. Remember to remember that. Sometimes it's hard to be heard or to let someone close and you don't have to be afraid just consult with God and He will help your heart be encouraged. It will also be rewarding to remember to never judge another, especially when we all sin and fall short of God's glory here and there, some more than others...so we shouldn't even have time to criticize when we have our own mirror to look into. Praying for each other sounds more fitting; that's what family does for family.

Family stands on a strong foundation so it doesn't crumble when the walls start to close in. True family will always stand together

Family doesn't gang up on other members.

Family will feud but it uses a respectable manner and remains open to a swift compromise because it is most concerned with each other's well being

Family isn't political, it is too humble to be and although no family is perfect (no human being is, for Jesus was the only perfect being to walk this earth and we would have never made it this far without Him), a real family will strive to be pure and it keeps God first which is as close to perfection that we can get

If you're really living and working for God, then it shouldn't be hard to separate yourself from satan fueled subdual like jealousy, pride, or grudges. A spirit filled with any of that cannot flourish and you're hurting yourself more than anyone else.

Yes family fusses and fights then falls to their knees before spewing hurtful words. Prayer keeps us together. Times will get harder and we can't do life alone so keep calling on our Father and relying on each other. Hold on and allow God to fight your battles since He says it is His to fight. God has a way of helping us see that all is okay and He promises victory to us when we follow Him.

2022 is gone and 2023 is in full effect. Try to be more and more thankful that you have another chance each day you wake up. The odds are not in our favor. Savor each moment; it wouldn't be wise to just let them pass by without being grateful. God sees all and can fix all so endure and do your part in making your church family what God envisions it to be. And although it is more beneficial, you don't have to belong to a church to have a church family. The church is in your heart so in gathering with other Christ believers you are a part of a family. God will carry us, let Him carry you and you too will get there.

A poem to the Lord called

"Someone Like You"

It's easy to say the words "I love you"

It's nearly impossible to prove that you love someone through every aspect of life but You make nearly, possible.

I'm unwrapping gifts with every word You say to me.

I'm blessed like I am a trillion men. Plus a million plus a million

All because of You

You're a dream that I could never have

There are no words descriptive enough for Your description

You never change. You don't ever need to

You give me all the inspiration I need

You tell me only what I should hear

You are never unfair

You're always there waking me up and seeing me to sleep

What You do to my heart no person no bullet no surgery no cardiac arrest can undo

Whenever I call, You answer. I could never get over on you

The most special impression You leave on me comes from the fact that I am so undeserving of Your kindness

I will try to love my most envious enemy as much as anyone I'll ever encounter

You have every answer to every question that has passed through my mind and You hold me

During my darkest days. You hold me then You make those days light

And I'm sitting here in tears because I'm just so overwhelmed with the notion that someone like You loves me

And You did way before I knew You

Epilogue

I want to be crystal clear without any misled or assumed ideas. I am the furthest person from perfection just like everyone else on earth.

Only in Christ can we be made pure.

So I am writing to myself as I am writing to the masses. I am putting into practice all portions of this book and I, King Rell, have a long way to go. Like the apostle Paul, I say, "what I'll do is forget what is behind and strive for what is in front of me, pressing on to the goal which is in Christ Jesus." (Phillipians 3:13,14)

Not only that, I struggle. I don't always live the Word that I read and that I teach. I stumble I fall short I fall I get back up again, I pray I fast I mediate and ask for help from God. I remember Ephesians 3:20 when it says:

We need not rely on our own power or perceived enough-ness; rather, let's rightly place our faith in the God who is able to do infinitely more than we can ask or think.

With that faith, and obedience to Him, God will pour out measures of power through love through wisdom through understanding by His grace, simply because He wants us to prosper.

I choose to remain humble. No matter what I accomplish or what I lack, I remain humble. Again I revert to Paul who in 1 Corinthians 2 says:

When I came to you, I did not come with eloquence or human wisdom as I proclaimed to you the testimony about God 2 For I resolved to know nothing while I was with you except Jesus Christ and Him crucified. 3 I came to you in weakness with great fear and trembling. 4 My message and my preaching were not with wise and persuasive words, but with a demonstration of the Spirit's power, 5 so that your faith might not rest on human wisdom, but on God's power.

I don't want to be like the world. I want to be like Christ. I want to do what God has put me here to do and not just for my own sake but for the sake of others I encounter and do life with. God's Word is a light to the path of a successful relationship of any kind. When two people in relations follow the Word, they can also grow together in it. Together they can seek ministry when dealing with problems. We have to always be open and honest. Pray together often.

Take quiet time away from each other as well in order to meditate and rejuvenate. Bring back the best you to the union. These ideas can be experienced in romantic, family, or friendly relationships because Christ is the solution to them all.

I'm interested in fellowship with other Christ followers where we can call upon the Holy Spirit to guide all of our decisions. We can't lose when we are led by God and it is important that we are for each other and even more so for those who are not yet in Christ. We are called to bring them in.

In Luke 12:8 Jesus said-

"I tell you, whoever publicly acknowledges me before others, the Son of Man will also acknowledge before the angels of God. 9 But whoever disowns me before others will be disowned before the angels of God. 10 And everyone who speaks a word against the Son of Man will be forgiven, but anyone who blasphemes against the Holy Spirit will not be forgiven."

It is my duty to talk about Christ and the thought of being acknowledged before the angels brings a leaping joy into my body!

Lastly I will acknowledge that the enemy has to know you. This is part of a walk with Christ. We must be so on fire for God that the enemy (satan) knows who we are and who we belong to. Take this example from Acts 19:13-

Some Jews who went around driving out evil spirits tried to invoke the name of the Lord Jesus over those who were demon-possessed. They would say, "In the name of the Jesus whom Paul preaches, I command you to come out." 15 One day the evil spirit answered them, "Jesus I know, and Paul I know about, but who are you?" 16 Then the man who had the evil spirit jumped on them and over-powered them all.

When your heart is right, when you truly accept Jesus and want Him to use you for His purpose, you will receive power to accomplish great feats. It's the way to the best life you can possibly have in this world...but when you are a pretender you will be exposed in the worst way. So I say to myself and I say to all who read this, don't just say you believe and want to be used by the Lord. Don't put on a show to impress people or fool others. It will be better for you to not serve God at all then to act like you do as a tool for manipulation. God bless you. May He bless us all

REFERENCES

Hebrews 13:3 Continue to remember those in prison as if you were together with them in prison, and those who are mistreated as if you yourself were suffering

Hebrews 13:8 Jesus Christ is the same yesterday today and forever

Psalms 1:2,3 blessed is the one who delights in the law of the Lord, and in His law meditates day and night. That person shall be like a tree planted by the rivers of water, that brings forth its fruit in its season, whose leaf also shall not wither; and whatever they do shall prosper.

Psalms 34:8 Taste and see that the Lord is good,

blessed is the one who takes refuge in Him

Psalms 82:6 "I said, 'You are "gods" you are children of the Most High"

Genesis 37, 39-49 the story of Joseph

John 8:36 so if the Son sets you free, you will be free indeed

John 14:6 Jesus answered *"I am the way the truth and the life. No one comes to the Father except through me"*

1 Corinthians 10:13 No temptation has overtaken you except what is common to mankind. God is faithful, and will never let you be tempted beyond what you can bear. When you are tempted, He also provides a way to endure it

Revelation 22:13 *"I am the Alpha and the Omega, first and last, beginning and end"*

Job 19:25-27 I know my redeemer lives and in the end I will see His face

1 Corinthians 1:31 Therefore, let the one who boasts, boast in the Lord

Matthew 8:27 The men were amazed and asked, "What kind of man is this? Even the winds and the waves obey Him!"

1 John 4:4 You, dear children, are from God

and have overcome them, because the one who is in you is greater than the one who is in the world.

Proverbs 3:27 Do not withhold good from those who it is due, when it is in your power to act

Song recommendations:

Thirsty (Reprise) by Marvin Sapp

Rivers Flow by Marvin Sapp

Job 31

"I made a covenant with my eyes not to look lustfully at a young woman. For what is our lot from God above, our heritage from the Almighty on high? Is it not ruin for the wicked, disaster for those who do wrong? Does He not see my ways and count my every step? If I have walked with falsehood or my foot has hurried after deceit- let God weigh me in honest scales and He will know that I am blameless-if my steps have turned from the path, if my heart has been led by my eyes, or if my hands have been defiled then may others eat what I have sown, and may my crops be uprooted. If my heart has been enticed by a woman or if I have lurked at my neighbor's door, then may my wife grind another man's grain, and may other men sleep with her; for that would have been wicked, a sin to be judged. It is a fire that burns to destruction. It would have uprooted my harvest. If I have denied justice to any of my servants, whether male or female, when they had a grievance against me, what will I do when God confronts me? What will I answer when called to account? Did not He who made me in the womb make them? Did not the same One form us both within our mothers? If I have denied the desires of the poor or let the eyes of the widow grow weary, if I have kept my bread to myself, not sharing it with the fatherless- but from my youth I reared them as a father would, and from my birth I guided the widow- if I have seen anyone perishing for lack of clothing or the needy without garments and their hearts did not bless me for warming them with the fleece from my sheep, if I have raised my hand against the fatherless, knowing that I had influence in court, then let my arm fall from the shoulder, let it be broken off at the joint; for I dreaded destruction from God, and for fear of His splendor I could not do such things. If I have put my trust in gold or said to pure gold, 'You are my security,' if I have rejoiced over my great wealth, the fortune my hands had gained, if I have regarded the sun in its radiance or the moon moving in splendor, so that my heart was secretly enticed and my hand offered them a kiss of homage, then these also would be sins to be judged, for I would have been unfaithful to God on high. If I have rejoiced at my enemy's misfortune or gloated over the trouble that came to him- I have not allowed my mouth to sin by invoking a curse against their life- if those of my household have never said, 'Who has not been filled with Job's meat?'- but no stranger had to spend the night in the street for my door was always open to the traveler- if I have concealed my sin as people do, by hiding my guilt in my heart because I so feared the crowd and so dreaded the contempt of the clans that I kept silent and would not go outside- oh that I had someone to hear me- I sign now my defense- let the Almighty answer me; let my accuser put His indictment in writing. Surely I would wear it on my shoulder. I would put it on like a crown. I would give Him an account of my every step; I would present it to Him as to a rule. If my land cries out against me and all its furrows are wet with tears, if I have devoured its yield without payment or broken the spirit of its tenants, then let briers come up instead of wheat and stinkweed instead of barley" the words of Job are ended

Made in the USA
Columbia, SC
22 June 2024

37168175R10043